# LOOK OU

# HEADHUNTERS!

冒

险

*Betty —*
*Thank you for*
*your faithfulness*
*throughout the years.*
*God Bless You.*

*Brandt Smith Jr*

*an extreme adventure in*
*missions*
*a collection of short stories*

by

*C. Brandt Smith, Jr*

C. BRANDT SMITH, JR.

Copyright © 2005
C. Brandt Smith, Jr.

**ISBN 0-9768020-0-7**

Printed in U.S. by Instantpublisher.com

"Therefore, go and make disciples of all the

nations, baptizing them in the name of the

Father and the Son and the Holy Spirit.

Teach these new disciples to obey all the

commands I have given you.

And be sure of this: I am with you always,

even until the end of the age."

***Jesus C., on a mountain in Galilee***

*Matthew 28: 19-20; NLT*


"Of course it's hard – but so was walking

up Golgotha.

But if we don't go, who will? These people need to

hear the Gospel."

***Alan S., on a mountain in China***

# *CONTENTS*

# PREFACE

# WHAT'S IN IT FOR YOU?

For you have been my hope, O Sovereign Lord,

my confidence since my youth.

From birth I have relied on you;

you brought me forth from my mother's womb.

I will ever praise you.

I have become like a portent to many,

but you are my strong refuge.

Since my youth, O God, you have taught me,

and to this day I declare your marvelous deeds.

Even when I am old and gray,

do not forsake me, O God,

till I declare your power to the next generation,

your might to all who are to come.

*Psalm 71*

What causes a sixteen-year-old boy to stand up in front of his entire church on a Sunday morning and announce, "God wants me to go to China and be a missionary"? I know now that only God causes that kind of courage to spring up in the hearts of his people.

If you grew up anywhere close to here or maybe a lot closer to 'there,' you'd get either an "Aww, isn't that precious? God bless that sweet boy." or a "Boy, you been out in the sun too long, ain'tcha?" Regardless of the reaction, the explanation is a supernatural one. If you believe God speaks today and still calls young people, guys and gals, into His service, you understand. The missionary call is one of the works of Holy Spirit.

God begins dealing with men and women at an early age. he grabbed me when I was fourteen. Some young people tune in much earlier that God is directing them to do something.

What is God doing?

What is His plan for our lives?

That's what this journey is all about, isn't it?

What you do need to know is that He does have a plan for your life. God has always been faithful to reveal His plan for me over the years. God has never left me dangling or wondering what His will is for me. By faith – as I have obeyed and moved forward – God has consistently guided and given me insight into His marvelous plan.

For I know the plans I have for you," declares the Lord, "plans to prosper you and not to harm you, plans to give you hope and a future. Then you will call upon me and come and pray to me, and I will listen to you. You will seek me and find me when you seek me with all your heart"

*Jeremiah 29:11-13*

It's as simple as that. Our role, our responsibility, our duty as Christians, our honor as ones who have been given such a precious treasure – is to be obedient. I know now that above anything else, God calls us to obedience.

Have you ever mumbled your way through the hymns in church that speak about obeying and following Jesus? You know the ones:

*"Wherever He leads, I'll go. Wherever He*

*leads, I'll go.*

*I'll follow my Christ, who loves me so –*

*Wherever He leads, I'll go."*

"I have decided to follow Jesus, I have decided to follow Jesus, I have decided to follow Jesus, no turning back, I'll follow Him…"

*Or how about this song,*

"Give me one pure and holy passion,

Give me one magnificent obsession,

Jesus, give one glorious ambition for my life

to know and follow hard after you…"

Have you thought about what that means? It's

about being obedient to the call of our Savior. Obedience can certainly take many forms and play out differently for different people. But know that when the Almighty Creator God of the universe says, "Hey, you. I want you. Get moving!" that there is only one response: getting it in gear.

And guess what? He is saying just that. No one is exempt from service. But there sure are many spiritual draft-dodgers snoozing in the churches, aren't there? Many people say they want to serve Christ. They make a public commitment, but fail to follow through. I've learned over the years that it isn't entrance into service that counts as much as performance. In other words, don't tell me what you're going to do—Show me!

The focus of this book is not about me. It never has been. The purpose of this book is to put in printed form the stories, the thoughts and the feelings I have experienced on the road less traveled. If some pages read like a journal, that's because they're straight out of a journal, written on the trail.

For me, taking that "road less traveled" has meant getting the Gospel of Jesus to a specific people group in China that had never had access to the message of salvation. I hope these stories paint a picture for you. I don't want you to read these stories and say, "Man, that guy sounds crazy! What a renegade!" I want your images to be in living color – pictures that scream out, "I can do this!"

C. BRANDT SMITH, JR.

## *The Road Not Taken*

*Two roads diverged in a yellow wood,*
*And sorry I could not travel both*
*And be one traveler, long I stood*
*And looked down one as far as I could*
*To where it bent in the undergrowth;*
*Then took the other, as just as fair,*
*And perhaps the better claim,*
*Because it was grassy and wanted wear;*
*Though as for that the passing there*
*Had worn them really about the same,*
*And both that morning equally lay*
*In leaves no step had trodden black,*
*Oh, I kept the first for another day!*
*Yet knowing how way leads on to way,*
*I doubted if I should ever come back.*
*I shall be telling this with a sigh*
*Somewhere ages and ages hence:*
*Two roads diverged in a wood, and I—*
*I took the one less traveled by,*
*And that has made all the difference.*
*-Robert Frost*

My desire is not to highlight myself, but to encourage you to look deep inside yourself and to listen.

What is your heart crying out for?

Are you striving for purpose in your Christian walk?

Are you frustrated and bored with what you're doing?
Are you tired of preaching to the choir?

Are you the choir?

Do you know that God is urging you to get out of your comfort zone, but you don't know how?

You don't know where?
Here's one suggestion: Find the most remote and least-reached people on the planet and become

their advocate, their bridge to knowing God through personal relationship with Jesus.

Read this book to see if it helps clarify anything for you. I don't particularly want to be an example for you, or to say, "This is what it's got to look like." When you finish this book, I want you to understand that to be a missionary does not mean putting aside fun, danger, or shelving the risk-taking lifestyle. To the contrary, it means dusting off these qualities and using them. If you don't have them, order up!

# Acknowledgements

Special thanks to my content editor, Russell Rankin, who was enormously helpful and who painstakingly listened to me telling these stories for hours. Russell traveled with me, camping out in tents along the China and Myanmar border, suffered weight loss and dehydration and sore feet. He is a trooper! I should also mention Angela, Russell's wife, for trusting me with her husband. I did return him only slightly used. Thanks Angela.

I also want to thank Gailia, my soul mate, wife and best friend. She turned me loose to chase after the things of God. She released me from my duties at home to be on the "edge" of where

God would take me. I could not share with you these mission adventures stories if she hadn't yielded her personal rights back to God and let me go.

Also, I want to thank my children, Justyn, Nathan, Whitney and Amber. They are real "MK's" (missionary kids). I've dragged them all over Taiwan, Thailand, China, Laos and Myanmar, and, best of all, they survived.

Another individual needs to be acknowledged on this page. Catherine Edgar, who read and corrected my grammar errors, thanks!

Finally, I want to thank my parents, affectionately known as Brother Curt and Ms. Jean. They taught me to say yes to God and His will for my life. I love you. Thank you for letting me be me.

Traveling up a river in China
on a bamboo raft looking for the Kawa

# INTRODUCTION

Delight yourself in the Lord
and he will give you the desires of your heart.
Psalm 37:4

John Maxwell said, "Each person's life story is written in risks—the ones taken and the ones avoided."

Being a missionary doesn't mean wearing a tie all day and talking in big theological words, either. I have some ties, and I know many of those big words. But those words and ties wouldn't get me anywhere in the area in which I work. In fact, they might get me killed. I can just imagine myself climbing up a mountainside in a suit and tie with a fifty pound pack of gear on my back. When I entered the village, everyone would be so interested in my clothing that they wouldn't hear what I said. This kind of scenario really happened years ago in China and on other mission fields. The Chinese nationals were so intrigued by the clothing missionaries wore, they rarely heard the message the missionaries were preaching. That's why missionaries like Hudson Taylor started wearing Chinese clothes. His message was more important than he was. Being a missionary on the edge means going through exhilaration and depression. Being a missionary on the edge means experiencing fear and sickness at times. Through the years I shall continue to speak and to encourage others to follow the less traveled trails.

Missions are real to me. I'm so passionate about missions that I am amazed that not everyone is on-board with what God is doing around the world. It grieves me when I think of people – young and old – who won't "let go and let God have His way in their lives." People sit in a church pew every week, bored to death and dying inside, just going through the motions. Authentic Christianity is about so much more than *you*, as the incident attests.

One evening after spending a long day speaking and making my "missions" presentation to a church in Northeast Arkansas, I had the most unique experience. I was standing at the back door of the sanctuary greeting people as they were leaving the meeting. Bill (not his real name) took hold of my hand and then hugged me. He was weeping and almost unable to talk. He must have held onto me for a minute or longer. When he finally regained his ability to speak, he told me the saddest story. His daughter wanted to be a missionary to an unreached people group. He spoke of her love for Jesus and her call to missions. "My daughter could have hiked and mountain biked into remote villages. She loved hardship and thrived on challenge," he said, choking back his tears.

"But my wife and I were so opposed to her going

off to some foreign country, that we didn't encourage her or support her decision in any way. As a matter of fact, we put up excuses and roadblocks in front of her to get her to change her mind. We told her she could do just as much good among less fortunate  people in her home state or county as she could in a far away place." His sad face became serious. "My daughter was killed in a car accident returning home from college," he said. "I wish we still had her. I wish she were alive and a missionary. I would rather have her alive and on the mission field than not to have her at all." I have had time to think about Bill and his change of attitude. The problem is that he is too late. His daughter was hindered from being where she felt

God wanted her. Bill realized his selfishness but lost the opportunity to encourage his daughter's obedient heart toward God's calling.

A couple of weeks later while ministering in another church, I was surrounded by a large group of older teenagers and college students after my presentation. Although some of the young people lingered to be friendly with the visiting missionary, others wanted to know the "how to" of getting on the field. These are the young people I love to invest my time and energy among. One young lady mentioned how God was calling her to the mission field. She spoke clearly and confidently. She sensed a genuine call on her life. Then she said, "My mother tells me I shouldn't consider going overseas. There is a lot to do at home."

Here was another young lady expressing her calling to leave home and go overseas, and her parents were placing doubt and roadblocks before her. All I could do was relate the story of Bill's daughter to her. I also asked her a question, "Did your mother and father dedicate you to the Lord when you were a newborn?" Very quickly she said, "Yes, they did." My counsel to her was to remind her mother and father – in love and submission – of the commitment they had made to God nineteen years earlier. I then said, "I'll be in prayer for you."

Five days later at a meeting of several churches, a woman approached me and introduced herself as the secretary for the Baptist Associational office. She then mentioned her daughter had heard me speak on obeying God's call to missionary service. I was expecting to hear a compliment from her because I thought the meeting had gone very well. Instead, I was shocked to hear her ask me to discourage her daughter. She actually wanted me to suggest to her daughter that God already had enough people serving overseas and that God didn't really need her. I was saddened by her attitude.

I replied in the same way I had counseled the 19-year-old the week before. "Did you give your daughter to God when she was a newborn?" I asked her.

"Yes," she said.

I further asked, "Have you reared your daughter in church where she has been regularly exposed to foreign missionaries and the instruction of the Great Commission?"

"Yes," she replied again.

Again I asked, "Did you send your daughter to

youth camps where she was regularly taught about missions and heard missionary speakers tell of God's work in a foreign land?"

"Yes. I did all that."

I then asked her: "Isn't it reasonable, then, that God would receive your gift and honor His word and call your child into His service?" She dropped her head. She really couldn't connect her offering and child rearing with God's calling. You see, parents who dedicate their children to the Lord and His work can and should expect God to call these children to Himself as they reach young adulthood. Don't play games with God. If the plans of your heart run contrary to your verbal vow to God, re-pent.

This book is not about me. It's not about any of us. It's about God. There is a huge world out there filled with people who have never heard the Gospel of Jesus Christ. With modern technology, the Internet, television, satellites, and newspapers, global barriers are surely shrinking. Today, the Gospel is beginning to reach into many previously untouched areas. These stories are about the areas beyond that. This is the world to which I have been asked to go.

But I'm just one person. To tell you the truth, I'm just an old guy. That's the name I go by, in fact.

The hard, on-the-edge world I work in attracts the younger crowd, for the most part. On one of the first hiking trips I led, I heard the "young Golden Gate Baptist Theological Seminary whippersnappers" calling me "S. O. Guy," instead of using my real name. "What's that supposed to mean?" I asked. "Is that some cool term you guys use these days, kind of like 'Mack Daddy' or 'Homie?'"

They laughed, and said, "No, it just means 'Some Old Guy.' That's what you are, but we love you."

Today, God is calling out a generation who are risk takers – young men and women who are not afraid to stand at the precipice and scream into the gorge beyond: "YES! I WILL GO! Whatever, however, and whenever – I choose to say 'Yes!'"

Go further. Go deep. Go with Him.

These are just my stories. Go make your own.

Blessings & Joy,

*S. O. Guy (C. Brandt Smith, Jr.)*

# CHAPTER ONE

## BEING ALIVE

The unpredictable mountain rains held back throughout the morning, resulting in a searing heat, gathering humidity like a sponge. The sky was clear and the mountains radiated with daylight. The village was dry enough for the women to begin spreading the freshly harvested mountain grain over the packed earth to dry in the sun. Other women hunched over homemade spools stuck in the dirt, deftly spinning homegrown thread. Nearby, the wizened old villager put down his tall, polished walking stick and squatted in the dirt by our group. His gaunt skin is tight around bony shoulders; creases of age and experience course his face. His skin is the color of dark honey, burnished from decades of exposure and experience. He is quiet but commands attention as if he is holding court.

Holding up his leathery fingers, he indicates he is seventy-eight years old. His ears are bad, he motions. His eyes, glazed by age and decades of wood smoke, seem blank and hollow. His expression changes, however, when our group of trekkers asks about the history and reputation of his people, historically known as headhunters.

"Yes," he reminisced with a hint of a smile – a

new light coming to his eyes. "We took heads." A respectful hush comes, as onlookers grow silent to hear his feeble voice, which strengthens with his smile. "I was twenty-four when I took a head," he says. "It was an argument over land. I caught him from behind." With another fierce grin, the old man drew an imaginary blade across his throat. No more explanation needed.

Kneeling on the ground beside him, I scratched a cross in the dirt and asked the gathered crowd of villagers if anyone has ever heard the name of Jesus. Responses were negative until the old man spoke again.

"When I was like this," he said, patting the head of a boy of about seven or eight, "white men came to our mountain, talking about Yesux *(Yesu)*. That was the only time."

Seek the Lord while he may be found.

Call on him while he is near.

Isaiah 55:6

A faraway look gleamed in his eyes. What it must have looked like at that time – a remote mountain in China, a fierce people group whose existence was built on fear, survival, human sacrifice – and a foreigner shows up on their mountain telling them about a God who gave His own life as payment for theirs? What was more shocking--seeing the pale stranger or hearing his message? Was he having a flashback? After all, here we stood, a group of light-skinned foreigners, giving his village the same message – more than seventy years later.

I knelt down beside the old man and looked him in the eyes. "God must love you very much for giving you another opportunity to hear about Jesus," I said.

Why had the Gospel's message been so long in coming to this village? What thoughts were racing through this old man's mind? Would God reveal himself today in this village? Would God's Holy

Spirit bring about salvation to these WA minority people who had waited so long?  I could only hope that this was the day salvation in Christ would be known among this village.

"Listen! Whoever is thirsty,

come to the water!

Whoever has no money

can come, buy,

and eat!

Come, buy wine

and milk. You don't have to pay;

its free!

Why do you spend money on

what cannot nourish you

and your wages on what does not satisfy you?

Listen carefully to me:

Eat what is good, and enjoy the best foods.

Open your ears, and come to me!

Listen so that you may live!

I will make an everlasting promise to you—

the blessings I promised to David.

I made him a witness to people,

a leader and a commander for people.

You will summon a nation that you don't know,

and a nation that doesn't know you will run to

you

because of the Lord your God,

because of the Holy One of Israel.

He has honored you."

"Rain and snow come down from the sky.

They do not go back again until they water

the earth.

They make it sprout and grow

so that it produces seed for farmers

and food for people to eat.

My word, which comes from my mouth, is like

the rain and snow.

It will not come back to me without results.

It will accomplish whatever I want

and achieve whatever I send it to do."

You will go out with joy and be led out in peace.

The mountains and the hills

will break into songs of joy in your pres-

ence,

and all the trees will clap their hands.

Isaiah 55:1-5 & 10-12

This is what it's all about. This is what brings the rush – the feeling of being purposefully alive. We had hiked and struggled across rugged mountainous terrain just for this purpose: to take part in the age-old, yet so simple, Biblical principle of sowing seeds of Truth on new ground. Sitting in the dirt surrounded by curious villagers, I picked up a short stick and began drawing – etching into the red clay earth pictures and words explaining the promise of God's redemption. Later, putting my arm around the village leader – a young man – I told him that the Kingdom of God had come near him today. He smiled and hugged me back. This divine moment almost didn't happen.

Just two days earlier, our small group of hikers had awakened from our first night being on the trail. The first day had been very hard – as first days usually are. We had jumped out on the trailhead at a small village and immediately headed uphill. Common logic says that after going uphill for a while, you will have the opportunity to go downhill. I don't think common logic has ever attempted to trek the lower end of the Tibetan Plateau in China, where the Himalayas taper off into the dense bamboo jungles of South China, Myanmar, and, ultimately, Thailand.

So uphill we went. The ground was hard red clay. Before us lay mountains unfolding into more mountains – each one cascading into the next, taking on deepening shades of gray-green shadow in the distance. Our plan was to hike the trail until it spit us out at the other side. Supposedly there was a small market town on the other end of the trail. At least the Chinese maps I had found showed that this was the case. But who could know for sure? I had never been here. My volunteer group – a band of six men – was putting their trust in me and a handful of possibly erroneous maps. I joked with them that I didn't know who was more stupid here – them or me. But this is partially what being on mission with God is about sometimes – knowing what we need to do and heading out into the wild unknown, trusting Him who is the ultimate Guide.

Our objective this trip was to find previously un-discovered settlements of this people group who traditionally hid high in the mountains. Where did they live? How big were their villages? What were their needs? By finding and mapping out details of these settlements, we would be laying the frame-work for future groups to come in and meet spe-cific physical and spiritual needs in the area. In our backpacks, my guys and I were also loaded with Gospel materials – tracts and cassette tapes pack-aged in Ziploc bags that we would distribute along the way.

For nine hours we climbed. The air was thin, and often we felt as though we were crawling at a snail's pace. As experienced as I was with this kind of hiking and terrain, I became worried as each hiker's water supply slowly dwindled. We had passed some locals along the trail. Of course they were shocked to see us, but I think it turned to humor once they began to examine us. We gave out some of our materials, which were happily received. These people had never held a Gospel message in their hands. Well, they'd never had a Ziploc bag, either.

Finally, as the sun began to shut the door on daylight, we crested a hill and found ourselves on the flat ground of a village's crop field. The people were warm and open to us – word had already seemingly floated up the mountain ahead of us that a group of foreigners was coming. After setting up camp on the rice terrace, we stretched our bodies, replaced our steamy boots with comfortable flip-flops, and fired up our camp stoves for a good hot supper. Some villagers came by, and I knew I needed to pay respects to the village elder, asking him formally for permission to pass through his village. Afterwards, a crowd of villagers greeted me at our campsite. A roaring fire was going, and the rest of the team was trying to communicate with the villagers using charades. Two of the villagers claimed to be Christians. They said no missionary had been there in nearly seventy years. We slept soundly that night.

The next morning we broke camp early to continue heading up the mountain. There was an eerie silence over the village as we headed out. Where was the laughter and friendliness from the night before? It felt like a scene from a Western movie when the bad guys stride down the dusty main street, and townsfolk retreat indoors, shuttering windows and flipping the 'We're Open' sign over in the barbershop.

We had walked approximately a mile when one of our guys turned and saw a jeep barreling up the mountain trail. How on earth a vehicle was making it up the trail that we walked, I don't know. But here it came. Blue plates are okay, I told them –

that would make it a civilian vehicle. White plates with red lettering means military – reason to get worried. The jeep came around the bend – blue plates. We continued walking, giving a friendly wave as they passed us. They stopped on the trail ahead of us, and four men got out. "Stop and talk with us," they said, casually. I explained we had a long way to go and did not have time to visit. Smile and keep walking, I told the team. The Chinese appeared flustered that we did not stop. Within a minute, we heard another jeep. The Beijing jeep had red letters on the license plate. This jeep was Chinese military. In seconds, we were completely surrounded by local authorities. Every one of these soldiers was fully armed with AK-

47's. This time, no one invited us to stop and chat. "Get over here and drop your bags," they barked.

We were herded to a level grassy area near the small village school. A crowd of people – the silent villagers – watched as we were told to cooperate. The village headman even showed up and stood nearby, looking smug. I smiled and greeted him warmly – selfishly hoping I was heaping coals on his head. I knew that he was the only man on the mountain with a cell phone. I wondered what type of financial kickback he was getting for turning us in? Backpacks were searched and the evangelistic literature and materials came tumbling out. Questioning began and the law was explained –

accusingly. WHAT YOU ARE DOING IS ILLE-GAL, they told me. These guys weren't just local hacks. The playing dumb tactic of "Oh, really? I didn't know that" wouldn't cut it with them. We were busted.

I was so proud of my team of volunteers. Everyone on the team was calm and very cool. Even though the military had weapons and we were caught with materials deemed contraband, I was able to keep the flow of humor in the conversation with the authorities and things went from being tense to only mildly tense – if there is such a thing. Our team photographer asked me if he could take some pictures of the events taking place for documentation purposes. I spoke very quietly to him and asked that he not do anything to make matters worse. However, he thought if he held the camera down low to his side, he could take a few pictures. The sound of his camera advancing film was too loud. The soldiers near him heard the winding sound and demanded his film. Thinking fast, he was able to switch rolls of film and gave an empty roll to the demanding soldier who had leveled his weapon at my photographer's body. I approached the soldier and my photographer and tried to defuse the tense standoff. Thankfully, God was so good. He gave me the words and the emotional response needed to calm the moment and nothing happened that would cause me to notify family members of an injury. Even within the edgy cat-and-mouse game, I knew God was at work. The soldiers continued to make us dig all our materials out of our bags, and they stacked them on the grass.

We had small battery-operated cassette players, bags of cassettes with Gospel messages, tracts, and Bibles all on display. One man in the group of authorities, who was not involved in hurling the intimidating questions at us, sidled over and picked up a Bible off the ground. He looked at it for a long time, and then opened it to the first page. His lips moved as he read Genesis 1:1, a truth that flies in the face of everything he had been taught in his atheistic, socialist upbringing: "In the beginning, God created the heavens and the earth." I wondered if he had been searching for meaning and sense to his life. I wondered if God was saying to him, "I created the heavens and the earth. It was I who created you."

We were loaded into the jeeps and driven back to the last town where we had started the day before. Talk about discouraging. What had taken us nine hours to climb the day before now took about 45 minutes – hurtling down at breakneck speed in a jeep. All our effort and struggle seemed lost. Back at the small village at the mouth of the trail, we found ourselves in custody. Questions were asked again; answers were given again. For what seemed like hours, we sat in the cement bunker-type building used by the authorities. One officer was left with us in the room. Although he was armed, he seemed more compassionate than the others. I negotiated our release more out of humor – telling the authorities that if they kept us, they would be responsible for housing and feeding us – and we were hungry and could eat a lot. I'm sure they were working hard on trying to get us off their mountain, as well. They didn't want to have to deal with us, either.

Finally, a rickety old minibus showed up, and they herded us out of town. This ride was cut short, though, by another group of police who pulled us over on the narrow mountain road. Where these people came from, I have no idea. These officers took down our passport numbers, names and visa numbers, rebuking me all the while for being a "spreader of the Gospel." I just smiled politely. Guilty as charged.  As we neared the next town, where we were ordered to get on another bus, go back to the provincial capital, and then get out of Dodge, I declared to the team that Plan "B" was now in effect. I asked the team, "What do you want to do?  Obey God or man? You came here to share the Gospel—what do you want to do?" Without exception, everyone on the team answered, "We want to share the Gospel!" My heart leaped with joy that day. I was surrounded with real men of God. I was reminded of Peter and John's witness as recorded in Acts.

They made Peter and John stand in front of them and then asked, "By what power or in whose name did you do this?"

They called Peter and John and ordered them never to teach about Jesus or even mention his name.

Peter and John answered them, "Decide for yourselves whether God wants people to listen to you rather than to him. We cannot stop talking about what we've seen and heard."

The authorities threatened them even more and then let them go. Since all the people were praising

God for what had happened, the authorities could-

n't find any way to punish Peter and John.  Acts

4:7, 18-21

As soon as the bus slowed, we shouldered our
packs and high-tailed it to the nearest trailhead.
This was still frontier territory, but I had been here
before. We would again go out in search of villages.  We spent the night camped next to a shal-
low creek that cut between a field and a steep hill.
Our whole team was giddy with excitement as we
recounted our thoughts and emotions from what
had happened that day. That night we rested well,
knowing that the next morning we would finally
encounter our target group.

This is why I'm alive, I thought that night, scrunched up in my tent beside my teenage son. As I tried to get to sleep, listening to the crickets in the field chirping in Chinese and the water dancing over the rocks in the streambed, my mind kept going back to our guard at the mountain station. Several times he told me, in an almost apologetic voice, "What you were doing was illegal. You shouldn't have done it." As we were leaving, he said it again. I faced him quietly and told him, "The kingdom of God has come near you today." He nodded and his eyes fell. "I know," he replied simply. "I know."

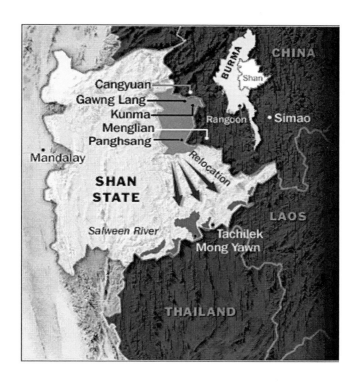

General region where the Kawa—

WA—Awa live

# CHAPTER TWO

# MY HERITAGE

Train a child in the way he should go,

and even when he is old he will not turn away

from it.  Proverbs 22:6

It was just a country church, and Sunday was a day when this part of Missouri seemed to stand still. Familieswould come right off their farms and off the trucks to come worship. Most would clean up pretty well–even if it meant just scrubbing the dirt off their hands really well, putting on a clean pair of overalls and combing their hair for the first time since last Sunday.

This was the kind of congregations Daddy always pastored. I can remember him going to a church in rural Missouri outside of Springfield. Of course the whole family went with him, and it was a trip of pure torture. That community was so rural and the ride was over the bumpiest, sorriest-excuses-for-roads that I've ever seen this side of China. We kids would arrive at church motion sick and smelling of vomit. More than once Dad had to pull the car over on the seventy-five mile trip to let us throw up. I'm halfway through my forties now, and I still get carsick. I think it may be God's joke on my life. If it flies, floats or has wheels, I'll be sick. And the thing is, that's what it takes for me to do what I do now.

The little church where my father first started preaching was in a place called Vanzant. I remember going home with church members on Sunday afternoons because the drive back to Springfield was so far. We'd just stay all day. My brother and I would run the hills and hollows of those Ozark Mountains all afternoon on Sundays. We'd swim in the summer and get covered with ticks and chiggers in the process. After getting cleaned up for night services, we'd settle in and listen to Dad preach the evening message. My dad was powerful in the pulpit. Every church he pastored grew, and we loved to hear him preach. When he preached, he never used phrases like, "I think," or "Maybe this means...." It was always, "God says...," or "This is the Word of God."

My daddy served in several churches, meaning that we'd move from time to time. When I was a kid, I didn't know what to think about that, although I knew that he was gone some Sundays. My mother's daddy – Grandpa Williams – was a circuit preacher. Back in the old days since preachers were harder to come by, especially in the more rural areas, Grandpa traveled around to surrounding communities and preached. He never learned to drive a car or ride a bicycle, so everywhere he went he walked, hitched a ride by train or used his thumb.

Grandpa Williams preached in rural churches and camp meetings all over Arkansas, Illinois and Missouri. We grandchildren would sometimes play under the church where Grandpa preached during the service. The floors were wood, and the cracks in the boards showed through. We could sit playing in the dirt in the crawl space underneath the floorboards and look up at Grandpa preaching. Some of the men and women chewed tobacco or snuff then, and they would spit down through the floorboards. Finding a place where we wouldn't get spit on during church was crucial for us kids.

The churches where Daddy served were mostly rural churches, too. Seems that every place we moved, the first chore was to install indoor toilets. The old wooden-framed buildings smelled of oak and pine. The wasps would dance off the ceilings and tap around the lights, and sometimes they would freefall from the high wooden beams all the way down to where we were sitting. Once a wasp dropped with the speed of a fighter jet from the ceiling to the floor right to the pew on which my mother and I were sitting. The wasp, after hitting the floor, flew right up my mother's dress. Well, she got up screamin' and a-hollerin' until the whole place looked more like a Pentecostal revival meeting than a Sunday evening worship service in a Baptist church. My brother and I were laughing so hard she had to send us out to get us to quit. There is just something special about hearing God's Word preached in an old wooden structure where the wasps fly around entertaining the children.

My dad was pastor and preacher first – then father.

As a kid, I didn't like that much, but now I understand it. As a matter of fact, sometimes I had to call to him by saying, "Bro. Curt" just to get his attention. Afterward he was Dad again. To the grandchildren he is "Pop." He was always strong and forceful and not ashamed to be the "spiritual leader" in our home. Bible readings were nightly. Many times we children were called back to the living room from our bedrooms for family devotions if we forgot. My father was raised without a dad, and he always would tell us children that God becomes a father to the fatherless. He said, "God became my father when my earthly father died." His dad died as a result of a car accident while taking the family to church one Sunday morning.

I became a Christian at the age of fourteen. By this

time my dad served as pastor of a larger county seat First Baptist church. I remember him and my mother talking about how they had given my brother, sister and me to the Lord when we were small and knew God had a plan for our lives. My family has had a special calling to serve the Lord. Several of my relatives are also in ministry. Some in my family are youth pastors and others are associate pastors, and we have worship leaders and senior pastors in our family as well. Because of this, it wasn't difficult for my family to hear me say that God was calling me, as well. Two years after I became a Christian – during a revival meeting – I felt called to missions, specifically China. No other place has ever had a hold on my heart like China. Mom and Dad were excited that God would use me and that I sensed a calling from God. Even with my statement that God was calling me to China, my parents never voiced any objection or disapproval.

Growing up, I was involved in all the typical things that young people do – football, track, and after-school jobs. But with everything else going on in my life, there was something that always rode with me in my heart, especially once I was in high school. I just knew God wanted me to be a missionary – plain and simple. I prayed and often told God I would go anywhere He wanted me to go. There's something incredible that happens when you do that. God answers. It wasn't long after I began telling God I would obey Him and be a missionary that He actually began telling me what He had planned for my life. I remember that day very clearly – going forward in the worship service where my father was pastor to inform the entire church of my "calling" to missions and to tell the congregation I was called to be a missionary in China.

Everyone was happy for me, but I knew that most people didn't really expect me to go to China as a missionary. After all, China was closed to missionaries. China was the land of the communists – a country so closed to the outside that we really didn't know anything about it. Most of what people knew about China was incredibly outdated, taken from older stories and books. China at that time was like the boogieman – this strange unknown force that was waiting to pounce on America. But missionaries had a history there, and I had read those stories. Some had even given their lives in blood for the Chinese people as they served God. I had one woman in the church tell me outright that I would never be allowed to go to China. My reply was, "God called me to China and if China is closed, then that is His problem." I knew God knew exactly what He was doing, and my earthly father also had a pretty good handle that God's word to me was true. It was a long way from Arkansas, though.

As an adult now, I feel good about standing in front of crowds of people – young and old-sharing about God and what a wonderful Savior we have. I feel comfortable in the understanding that I am a messenger, just as my father and my grandfather were. But as confident as I feel, it so often makes me stop to think about the man who molded me and influenced me more than any other person. Dad's love for Christ and his confidence in the written Word have encouraged me to be faithful in my walk with Christ and my ministry, as well. My dad told me not long before he died that something must be in our blood, since I'm doing the same thing as a missionary that he did and my mother's father did – never sitting still, never seeing the end of the road, in a way. I guess my daddy was right. There's another village over the crest of the next mountain.

# C. BRANDT SMITH, JR.

Volunteers and young WA at our campsite

# CHAPTER THREE

## THE PEOPLE I LOVE

## ARE THEY WORTH IT? YES!

the earth shook,

the heavens poured down rain,

before God, the One of Sinai,

before God, the God of Israel.


Why gaze in envy, O rugged mountains,

at the mountain where God chooses to reign,

where the Lord himself will dwell forever?

Psalm 68:8 & 16


High on the mountains of China, two men struggle

on a hillside terrace cut into a steep peak. The argument begins to turn violent with the two men pushing and shoving. Finally, punches are thrown. Within moments the shoving match turns into a struggle for life. Only one man will walk away from that plot of ground. The other will die. He will lie motionless, looking up at his enemy as his blood flows from his body. With one decisive blow, the Kawa man is dead. The WA who remained had his own wounds to tend, but at least he was still alive. He was alive, but for how long?

Fear of retaliation soon spread through the WA village. News of a killing, even a killing in self-defense, seemed to travel quickly between the remote, rustic villages tucked within the mountains. It was as though the news was carried on the wings of the mountain birds. As the news of the Kawa man's death reached the Kawa village, anger and hatred welled up in the other Kawa men. The calls for revenge by the villagers became louder and louder. Meanwhile, in the WA village, fear and concern grew with every minute. The WA villagers knew it was only a matter of days, perhaps hours, before the Kawa warriors would descend from their village, fueled by a rage that would demand vengeance.

The Kawa enjoyed the higher elevations. From cloud-covered peaks they could rain terror on their neighbors and maintain a somewhat dominant status over the other tribes in the area. They were proud of their headhunting and boasted about the "taking of heads." Soon the Kawa did come down into the WA village, like a tiger attacking its prey. Screams went up from every WA home. Blood was spilled that day, and every family claimed a loss. The heads of more than seventy men were taken in exchange for the one life of a Kawa man.

A few years ago, I was in the village where this raid had taken place. Though the event had taken place thirty years earlier, it still burned in the hearts and minds of these WA. As I sat and listened to an eyewitness tell this story, it seemed as fresh in his mind as if it had happened earlier that week. Some twenty years after the bloody battle, the man told me, his WA village had heard the Gospel, and by 1985 most had received Jesus Christ as their Savior. A church now stands on the high place in the village where black magic and animistic spirits had once been worshipped out of fear. A Bible and an arrangement of plastic flowers now lay on a small wooden table used for the Lord's Supper. A work of God's grace had transformed this place.

As for the fierce Kawa up on the peaks, shrouded by the mountain mists, they are still lost – having never heard the Gospel of Jesus Christ. The Kawa haven't experienced God's grace. Part of the reason has to do with their location. They live in the summits of the mountains, in villages nestled in clearings, terracing fields out from the red clay of the mountains. The elevations pose a huge challenge for anyone trying to carry the message of God's plan for mankind to the hidden people of the mountains.

As I began to ask more questions about the Kawa, the WA storyteller suggested he could guide me to the Kawa village where the Gospel had not penetrated. How amazing is that? What a tremendous testimony and faith this man showed me. Imagine a WA believer willing to go to the Kawa who murdered so many in his village. I became convinced, right then and there, that the Kawa would be reached with the gospel. It also became so clear to me that the surrounding WA villages –where Jesus is known – would play a huge role in reaching these fierce people.

One of the first times I attempted to make contact with the Kawa, I traveled around putting together as much information as I could about their location, their way of life and the conditions of their existence.  Hiking through WA villages on the lower slopes, I asked the people to tell me where the Kawa lived. Over and again, I was told: "Further up the mountain." In addition to that, I began to get more and more understanding of just how feared the Kawa were. The other Wa never ventured near the Kawa villages; the Wa would say, "Ta men hun xong, ta men xia wo men (They are fierce. They will kill us.)"

I praise the word of God.

I trust God.

I am not afraid.

What can mere flesh {and blood} do to me?

Psalm 56:4

The mountain areas the Kawa call home are a sub-tropical climate with plenty of rainfall, which makes it suitable for crop cultivation. These mountains are also rich in mineral resources like gold, silver, tin, copper, aluminum and timber. Because of the poverty of the mountain people, they lack the necessary tools to mine or properly extract anything of value. I saw people using shovels, picks, and explosives to blast out the sides of mountains. Very dangerous work – with little reward for the effort.

There may be other reasons that the Kawa come across as fierce and isolated. To a large degree, they isolate themselves and come across as menacing and unfriendly because of their low self-image. The Kawa are considered the "black" skinned minority group. This is understandable for a people who spend most of their time outdoors in the bright mountain sun. While the Kawa may actually be darker than other people groups, their skin is further baked a deep brown by the sun. Because of this perception they seem to be looked down upon, but they also seem proud of their fierceness. This is partly due to the treatment they have received from the Han Chinese and other fairer-skinned minorities. I can't remember how many times a Kawa has said to me, "we are the ugly people." It has been my joy to tell them that God created them in His image, and they are not ugly, but beautiful.

Life is hard for the Kawa, and anything but comfortable and peaceful. For centuries, the animistic mountain-dwellers took the heads of their enemies to appease their gods and to ensure a good crop. Early each year during the months of March, April and May the WA (Kawa) took heads, from distant enemy or nearby neighbor villages, to sacrifice to the evil spirits. They gave priority to a head with a thick beard, believing that their crops would then grow thick like the man's beard. I gave a nervous chuckle the first time I was told this, and clutched my throat while stroking my hairy cheeks. The custom of taking heads for harvest blessings kept each village in a state of preparedness, never knowing when it would be attacked or its members ambushed along the roadway.

Honor and prosperity came through spilled blood, a rite reflected in their traditional saying: "There is no sight so beautiful as the three-pronged fork" – the instrument used to hang the heads of their victims. Heads mounted in the villages and headless torsos dragged through the fields were believed to bring honor and prosperity to the clan, but bitter feuds between enemy tribes could drag on for generations. The WA people are also well known for their practice of headhunting, which is rumored still to continue today in some of the remote parts of Myanmar's Shan State, also known as the WA Bang or WA State. An integral part of the sacrifice ceremony was the beating of a special wooden drum, which only the chief or the witch of the village was allowed to use. This drum was regarded as holy and was built in accordance with strict religious regulations. Many of the WA villagers worshipped this wooden drum, believing that it called the spirits back from the dead. It was also used to assemble the men prior to war or a fight.

The demons that grip these people demanded the sacrifice of humans to assure the crops will not fail. As I researched the Kawa, I began to find more stories of their heritage, all painted with a blood-soaked brush. In 1962, for example, a WA man from Daigela village of China's southern Yunnan Province cut off a person's head by mistake while working in the fields. The victim's village retaliated by cutting off the heads of more than sixty people from Daigela. Incidents like this in the past usually sparked a continuing sequence of killings that could last for generations – a bitter Hatfield versus the McCoy feud – with the loser losing his head. In 1936 the WA of Zhongke butchered more than one hundred households in the Ximeng Mountains of China. Only three people were able to escape. The booty of severed heads was transported back in the loaded saddlebags of eight cows.

The Kawa are more bound spiritually than the other WA groups. Their mixture of black magic and Buddhism holds a powerful grip over them. As I conducted my research, I observed a great deal of animistic practices, but it can all be summed up by describing these people as being held in fearful bondage to the spirit world. During one trip among the Kawa, I asked my host as politely as I could about their religion and whom it was they actually worshipped. I learned some amazing things that evening and had a hard time sleeping because of the images that came into my mind. The god who is worshipped is called Awa Sheng Di – the god of the WA. Awa Sheng Di is a god who is feared and can be approached only one time a year. My host told me all this over our simple meal of steamed rice, vegetables and hot tea. He motioned over to a door off the room we were in. The god lives in a room set aside in the home where the family enters just once a year to make their offering. Not to offend this god, the worshipper leaves the room quickly, shutting the door until the next year. The fear associated with this god is very great.

Despite their reputation of fierceness and fury, the Kawa have very tight family relationships, and several generations usually share a dwelling. For the most part, adults seem to be monogamous, and showing deference and respect to the elders of the village is very important. It is not unusual for families to have large numbers of children due to the infant mortality rate. Many of the villages are suffering because of the lack of adequate medical services, and the small children suffer the most. The love and unity felt within WA, Awa and Kawa families was obvious. In one particular village, a

Kawa man was visibly emotional as he told me how five of his nine children had died.

The typical house in a WA or Kawa village is made from bamboo and palm leaves. The bamboo serves as structural support and is split and somewhat shredded to then be woven into walls. Palm leaves or blades of grass are tied together and tightly placed to shed water during the rainy season. In the homes, floors are usually dirt, or in some cases the houses sit up off the ground, which allows for bamboo flooring. Either floor, dirt or bamboo supports the cooking area – a fire in the middle of the floor. This fireplace is simply a small campfire-sized cooking area where all the cooking takes place. It is also the place where tea is brewed and conversations take place.

Sipping my tea and looking around the sparse, dark house, curiosity got the best of me, I admit. I just had to check this worship room out. With my host's hesitant permission, I peered into the room. It was dark and musty. Cobwebs covered every corner, and the walls and a simple offering shelf were caked with dirt and residue from past offerings. Dried blood was all over the floor. The darkness was pervasive. "I wouldn't want to go in there, either," I thought. No wonder these people would do their business and hightail it out of the room. It gave me such a renewed appreciation for the loving kindness of my God and King.

As for being receptive to the Gospel, I was always told that the WA, Awa and Kawa have remained staunchly opposed to the Gospel and have threatened those who have dared to approach their settlements. As of July, 1998, there were no known Christians living among them. Since the Kawa are residing in a restricted access area, they have been shut off from outside missionary influences. I've come to understand and believe that they may not be as opposed to the Gospel as previously believed; they simply have not had access to it. That is what grips me and shakes me to the core. How will they know if no one tells them?

Then Samuel said," Is the Lord as delighted

with burnt offerings and sacrifices

as he would be with your obedience?

To follow instructions is better than to sacrifice.

To obey is better than sacrificing the

fat of rams.

1 Samuel 15:22

But our God is a God of wonders, and I know that God desires to move among the Kawa in the same manner that He made Himself known to the WA, the close cousins – and frequent blood enemy – of the Kawa. It was 1906 when God chose to reveal Himself to the WA through an amazing and miraculous course of events.

Despite never having heard of Jesus, WA "prophets" began speaking out messages similar to John the Baptist, telling the people to forsake their headhunting and violence, and to prepare their hearts for the arrival of the True God, Siyeh. At that time a witch doctor or Shaman in a certain WA village owned three white donkeys. He laid his hands on the middle donkey and told the village elders, "If you follow this donkey, it will lead you to the true God." For weeks the elders followed the donkey for a distance of two hundred miles across remote terrain. One day it stopped outside the house of William Young, an American Baptist missionary who was working amongst the Lahu tribe. Young became the first to take the Gospel message to the WA. Salvation swept many areas as hundreds of hearts already prepared by the Holy Spirit converted to Christ.

Despite being surrounded by groups of other Christians – some numbering in the thousands – the Kawa have remained staunchly opposed to the Gospel and have threatened those who have dared to approach their settlements. The Kawa are more bound than the other Wa groups, their mixture of black magic and Buddhism proving a powerful hold over them.

Yet they say to God, 'Leave us alone!

We have no desire to know your ways.

Who is the Almighty, that we should serve him?

What would we gain by praying to him?'

Job 21:14-15

Still trapped in extreme poverty and rugged isolation, these people will only hear the gospel through the sacrificial lives of obedient Christians. The focus for doing this is not just to trek out past our comfort zones, our culture, and our civilization to sit in their villages. If that were the case, missions would be nothing more than a glorified field trip. We would be nothing more than a group of people trying to take it one step beyond what the *Lonely Planet* guide has to offer. While we can do that and take people out to these far-flung places, our focus must be based on the passage in the book of Revelation where every tribe, tongue and nation is worshiping before the throne of God. That is the end result, and that is what we should focus on – not the sweat, the aches, the danger, or the peaks imposingly standing in front of us. It's about Jesus. Doing it for any other purpose is a waste of time – neatly wrapped in a waterproof Gore-Tex shell.

# CHAPTER FOUR

# VISITORS IN THE NIGHT

The Tibetan Plateau is a long strip of steep, craggy mountains that taper off from the Himalayas, trickling down all the way into northern Thailand. It's steep. I was leading a handful of hikers – volunteers who had come out to help me work in some of the remote villages. This actually took place in the Peacock village. We were spending the night in a mud brick school building. We had made our way into the WA Bang of Burma. It was frightening because this was the area where my son Justyn and I had been held hostage for three days the year prior to this visit.

No tents tonight – our team was beat. We would sleep in the schoolhouse. Our sleeping, however, was so uncomfortable because the fleas and the mosquitoes were more than plentiful. We all used Deet and other insect repellents, but these bugs seemed unaffected.

The only thing worse than the insects buzzing around was the air I felt from the wings of the bats as they ate mosquitoes and gnats just inches from my face.

It was about 11:00 p.m. when we were startled awake by loud voices counting off the number of our team members in the Thai language. I was totally unprepared for what was about to happen.

"*Nung!*" (one!)

"*Song*!" (two!)

"*Saam*!" (three!)

"*Sii*!" (four!)

"*Ha*!" (five!)

"*Hok*!" (six!)

It was eerie. I was further jarred awake in the darkness by the gripping pain of an army boot – and the foot that WAs in it – that jammed on my thigh to hold me down. Fully aWAke, I found myself looking into the barrel of an AK-47 and being kicked by a soldier. If you've never had the unique wet-your-pants opportunity to stare down the barrel of an AK-47, let me just assure you: the barrel of an AK-47 is round. Its gunmetal gray color glistened in the light of the dim flashlights held by some of the soldiers.

Looking around in the darkness, I could see other soldiers, dressed in full combat gear; all armed to the teeth, locked and loaded standing, over my team. The soldier standing on my leg continued kicking me with his other boot. *"Bhood Thai dai mai?"* Do you speak Thai? he demanded. *"Pom bhood Thai dai, nit noi,"* I answered, telling him I could speak a little.

Our passports were confiscated, and for two hours I was questioned about why a group of dirty Americans were sleeping in their schoolhouse, on their mountain. What I didn't know was that war had broken out again in a nearby area between some Thai soldiers and the WA-Burmese military. There was really no way we could have known that. We hadn't exactly been on the information superhighway the last few days, and this type of activity didn't really show up on many headline news stations. It's pretty front-page news when you're staring down a gun barrel, though; that's for sure.

As I was allowed to rise to my feet, I spoke in Mandarin to the United WA States Army soldiers. I began to explain our purpose and that I was a missionary. No need to avoid stating our real purpose. I shared the Gospel with those soldiers that night hoping it would bring some kind of calm to a very tense situation. One of the soldiers recognized me as the man with the Bibles who had visited them a year earlier. He said to his commander, "This is a good man. He loves our people. He gave us Bibles and prayed for us last year." As soon as he spoke these words, the order was given to lower the firearms. I sighed a prayer of thanksgiving, and God gave me the verse I had learned and recited often,

"Even when I am afraid, I still trust you."

Psalm 56:3

This was my first trip back to this area in nearly a year. It was an area within our people group where I knew it was only a matter of time before God would start moving among the remote villages in those mountains. Someone just had to get the message of Jesus to the WA, Awa and Kawa. It was I!

China has more than one billion people, the majority of whom are Han Chinese; these are the Chinese who pretty much run the country. In the background, though, are millions of others belonging to other minorities. Many of these groups of people still cling to ancient traditions and ways of doing things – usually because of poverty and pride – and are fiercely independent. The Awa, one of the smaller groups, are no different. God broke my heart for the Awa a long time ago, and ever since then my heart has been focused on winning the Awa for Jesus. These people have historically been a fierce headhunting people. In some remote villages, I'll still come across an old man who has taken the head of his enemy. Today, they are feared by other minorities – who really don't want to have anything to do with them and are afraid of them. Their fierce reputation sticks. These folks are also the opium producers and smugglers of China and Myanmar. Put all that together, and there's a pretty good chance that if you meet an Awa, he'll have a gun nearby. If he's too poor, it'll be a machete – but no less deadly.

A few years ago, my teenage son Justyn and I hiked our way into this very village where the Awa still produce opium. The people were suspicious – thinking we were from a drug-busting agency coming in to break up their livelihood. For three days we weren't allowed to leave. We knew that was an opportunity from God, so we presented the gospel and shared our testimonies. To some of the Awa who could read, I gave copies of God's Word, the Book of Psalms; to others we gave audiocassette tapes with Awa messages. One man truly warmed up to us and showed us hospitality. To me, that's an invitation to come back. His name is Ai Blung. He is our man of peace. For two nights and three days, we demonstrated God's love and witnessed to these fierce people, and on the third morning we were allowed to leave.

It was to this same village that I returned with a group of five volunteers the next year. In God's faithfulness, the same "man of peace," Ai Blung, met us and fed us a meal. But unlike the year before when my son and I were treated with suspicion, this time we made it into the main part of the village. My second born son, Nathan, was with me this time. We had spent the night in the mud brick schoolhouse in the middle of the village. That evening, we built a big campfire on the slopes of the mountain next to the school. We told Bible stories, and several of the volunteers shared their testimonies. The crowd listened very carefully to our words. We told them how God had changed our lives and had called us to be in this village. The people listened intently. There was no visible move, but they all listened and heard the Gospel.

As we prepared for sleep our team prayed for our host – the man of peace who had taken us in. He had not only protected my son and me on the first visit but was also taking care of us on this visit. We knew God would do something powerful here.

What we really didn't have a full understanding of was the political trouble that was brewing all around us. The areas all around where we were sleeping were now on full alert and teeming with bands of soldiers. To this group of soldiers in the middle of the night, they had stumbled on the mother lode. Surely we were a band of covert CIA operatives sneaking around the rebel areas, infiltrating and gathering information to break the back of the rebel troops once and for all. The commander of this small force was not convinced otherwise. Our passports were confiscated, and we were held in a tight ring, guarded by camouflaged soldiers. One of the members of that team asked, "What do we do now?"

"Pray," I told my team, as if I really needed to remind them of that.

It's always so beautiful in times of need when God cracks through a little. It's not that He can't split the whole problem open right then and there – it's just a reminder to us, probably for the same reason Jesus called his disciples men "of little faith." It's just a glimpse of His hand to tell us to relax a little. That's exactly what He did.  One of the soldiers who had been guarding the perimeter of our campsite stepped up. Up to that point, no other soldier had really said anything. But he recognized me from my first visit to the area nearly a year before. We must have gone through his village.

"Mr. Shr is a good man," he said to his commander, using a name that I am sometimes called in this area. "He is a missionary, and he gave me a Bible last year. He is completely trustworthy."

With those words, for the first time all night, the guns were dropped and slung across the backs of the soldiers. That was the glimpse. God said, "Hey, relax. I've got this."

The officer in charge still kept our passports. I was concerned that he might take them to another officer. I challenged him to return them. He said he would, and I demanded them back by seven the next morning. The officer then said he wanted me to go to drink beer with him. I told him I was a missionary and a pastor and wouldn't drink.. Before disappearing with our passports, he said I should buy beer for his men. I basically told him that if our passport "processing" was done quickly, I could pay a small "processing fee."

I told the team what was happening and suggested a prayer meeting. So, we all prayed quietly for the next hour or so. My prayer at that time was simple, "God, you don't need me or this team to do your will in this place. But, you have given me the burden to reach these people. Until you remove the burden, I'll keep showing up for the spiritual battle." Committing to show up here again and again is not a light statement. In this area, the military often shoot trespassers and foreigners on sight. It was dark and frightening. The team just prayed. It is one thing to say, "I trust you, God," but quite another to actually put your life into His hands and prove it. This volunteer team trusted God. I saw that demonstrated that night.

Approximately two hours after the passports and

the soldiers disappeared, they returned again. The commander, flanked by two soldiers in full combat gear, faced me in the light of a small flashlight. "You are a good man," he said. "We want you here. You and I will have a great friendship. I welcome you anytime to this place." With that said he handed me the six passports, told me to relax, and shouted the command to stand at attention. His soldiers stood at attention and all three saluted me. I stood there and solemnly saluted them back as they melted back into the dark night.

Everyone always asks me whether or not I bought the soldiers their booze. When the soldiers returned with our passports, they reminded me that I had promised them some money. While some may see this as a bribe, and others may see it as my buying them beer, it did secure our passports. One of the guys who was hiking with me that night told me some time later that the wife of the missions pastor at his church dislikes me to this day for having paid a bribe to the soldiers. All I can say is that I would have given him a lot more money if I thought it would have kept my guys from getting shot that night. I doubt that minister's wife would have complained had her husband been on that team that year. We had a good laugh about the situation, because these are my friends, and we have shared many moments where we were challenged to do things "differently."

One of the most beautiful moments happened after the soldiers left us that night. We were left there in the dark, hearts pounding – hearts that were turned to God rejoicing for the way He took care of us. We had totally forgotten about the mosquitoes and fleas. We really needed to get to sleep – we had a few hours of darkness left, and we really needed to hit the trail and get out of this village as soon as we could the next morning. But who could sleep at a time like that? We were so energized with adrenaline that we just lay in the quiet, practically hearing the blood rushing and pounding in our veins. I had my sleeping bag on the ground beside a guy we called Tucker. Tucker had been out trekking with us a couple of times, including the time the authorities hauled us off the mountain. He was only about twenty years old. In the quiet of the night, Tucker scooted over to me on the ground. "Guy," he whispered, "I think this is where God wants me to spend my life." That statement blew me away. Here was a young man who had left the comforts of America to trek the unknown and who literally an hour before had had a machine gun pointed at him now responding with the realization that God was calling him to a life of service in such an environment. That was an extremely humbling moment for me. I am so grateful to God for the way He moves in the hearts of men. God did a great work that night on the mountain and continues to open doors for us in this area. It's incredible to think that now there are more than 2000 believers in that area who have been baptized and are receiving discipleship training and meeting in house churches. We now have access to 400 villages, 100,000 AWA in that region. God has been very good to us.

This would be our fifth trip into the WA State for the purpose of making contact with the people of the Peacock and Mushroom villages. The first time I attempted this contact my son Justyn and I were not allowed to leave on orders from the "head-man." He was also the local warlord. After three days we were allowed to leave. The second time I made contact with the Peacock village, WA soldiers awakened our team from our sleep at 11:30 pm. They treated us roughly until one of the soldiers recognized me as a missionary. I talked with the soldiers who had me looking down the barrels of their AK47 weapons.

The third time into this village I had brought a medical team with me. We treated every sick and ailing person. Our dentist, doctor and pharmacist met many physical needs that day. I also presented the gospel to the village. It was new information.

The fourth trip into the area was at a time when I was traveling elsewhere. I sent two team members and my fifteen year-old daughter. They were warmly received and were able to set up the next medical team's visit. We had just returned from this fifth visit. It was better than we could have imagined. The neighboring village had us set up a clinic for them, too. We treated many people there. The team was able to teach Christian WA songs to the people and to show the Jesus-film. We saw God tear down strongholds.

The first day into the village, our man of peace, the local schoolteacher introduced me to the village elder. I didn't remember this man. It turned out he was the warlord that had held Justyn and me for three days two years previously. I felt my anger rise as I began to realize with whom I was meeting. This time he was warm and friendly. I gave him my favorite pen and my only bag of coffee. I should say he requested my pen and coffee. I didn't want to give him anything except a punch.

He told me he would need to go to the WA authority and request permission for us to be in his village. I didn't know how that would go. However, later that night as I lay in my hammock trying to settle in for the night, teacher Ten came to let me know we were really welcome to stay and do our clinic. Before bed that night we had shown the J-film to a room full of people. There were so many people in the WA house I feared it would collapse.

After a few hours I told everyone to go home, and I would show the film again the next day. We did- -to a standing-room-only crowd in the mud-brick school. The small children were sitting in the rafters while the bigger kids and adults were watching the J-film below them. These poor, estranged-from-Christ villagers had warmly received us. Our team of volunteers saw the God of the Book of Acts work that day. I was reminded of His awesome power and ability to protect, remove fear and give me boldness in the middle of my own inadequacies. We would have never seen the sick receive aid and the curious learn about Jesus if we hadn't persevered. It was a difficult journey.

The team consisted of one sixty-five year old medical doctor who was on his second journey with me. Our nurse was a woman in her forties, and her husband was a tall man who weighed 275 pounds. Both of these individuals showed great love for my people and demonstrated a desire to be on the team. They suffered greatly.

Our nurse suffered two anxiety attacks early in the hike. We were very concerned for her health. Her husband had been hospitalized twice for heat exhaustion, and at one point was on the verge of suffering another episode of over-heating. He found a nice clear stream of water and lay down for nearly an hour, letting the water rush over his body to bring his temperature down.

Several times the mountains were so steep that Nathan, my son, had to make multiple trips up and down the mountain carrying the backpacks of the other team members. My son was such a benefit to the team and me. His language ability and skill in hiking and ministering to the needs of the team really were a godsend. The trails were also dangerous. Several times we approached areas that were washed away by the rain. In at least three places the trail became a stream and was muddy. Two or three of the team slopped through the mud and soaked their shoes. Everyone had blisters on his feet. I was able to loan my Gortex socks to our Hong Kong personnel. He had not purchased boots, but only wore tennis shoes.

At the second village we were received with much enthusiasm. It was here where we had held a previous clinic. The people came and saw the doctor and nurse. People needed medicine and treatment for intestinal problems, back aches and skin problems. We treated several cuts and abrasions. At one point I looked up to find some well-dressed men watching us work. They were very curious and were also able to read the labels on the medicine bottles. I learned they were drug smugglers from Guang Xi, Guang Dong and Yunnan provinces.

At this time, my team leader and I began to preach the Gospel. The clinic came to a quiet hush. We preached a simple message in Mandarin and in WA. When I gave the invitation twelve to fifteen men accepted Christ as their savior. Unsure if they really understood, we repeated the Gospel. Again they said, "We want Jesus."

We estimated that we treated approximately 200

men, women and children in those two clinics. The greatest impact will be for all eternity; salvation had come to several men that day. Within thirty minutes things were back to clinic status. Treatment resumed and people were receiving assistance with their medical concerns.

Several military soldiers who had mysteriously appeared caught my attention. I learned they were the bodyguards to a Dr. Wei. Dr. Wei is the primary government official in the WA State for the Long Tan district. He watched with great interest as we treated the sick and gave medicine to the people. Later, he also requested treatment for a headache. Our doctor placed his acupuncture needles into the face and neck of this government official. The bodyguards also complained of illness.

We treated all of them and prescribed medicine for them to take away. Dr. Wei was so encouraging to us that he invited us to return with him to his clinic. We declined for our time was up. However, I planned to return the next week with a team and to visit his clinic. My goal is to set up future medical teams to work in the WA area among the poorest and least evangelized villages.

Our team had a great experience. They saw firearms and AK47's and soldiers, the likes of whom they had never seen before. The elements of adventure and risk drive many of my volunteers, but the highlight was watching Jesus work in the hearts of those men during the Gospel presentation. They'll never be the same. Nor will the team.

121

Mountain view in the WA State

## CHAPTER FIVE

# CHRISTMAS IN THE EXTREMES

A few years back, our team had an amazing Christmas that none of us will forget. We planned something called "Operation Saturation" – we were going to hike around and distribute CDs and films in the local language that explained what Christmas is all about. Surely, we thought, hardly anyone has heard of Christmas in these areas. But think what an impact it makes coming in to a place and introducing Jesus to someone for the first time. The true meaning of Christmas is right there – freshly drawn on a clean slate.

What follows is in journal format written by one of the guys who headed up the trip, giving a day-by-day; blow-by-blow account of team's amazing Christmas, and how it really turned out a little different from what we had all expected.

## Dec. 24—second day out

We took another "hell on wheels" bus ride for six hours to the trailhead that one of our teammates recognized from a previous scouting trip. We got off the bus around 2:00 p.m., got our gear together, and headed out up the mountain. A couple hours later, we came across the first village. We were simply going to drop some material and leave, but the people received us more warmly than any place I'd ever been before, and they practically forced us to stay. It turns out that nearly this entire village claims to be believers, and they had already started celebrating Christmas!

They had built their own meeting place, and about one out of every five people had his own hymnal written in his own language using a phonetic system. As far as I can tell, they were probably translated by Vincent Young about 60-70 years ago. Vincent Young is the first and only other missionary to have walked among these people. It's amazing to come across a remnant of something he left behind, and even more amazing to meet some really old dude who remembers seeing him.

Since this was a holiday time, they met together for prayer and singing about five times a day. No lie – at least five times a day. Of course, we knew many of the tunes, and we sang right along with them, but with our English lyrics. They also had a time of prayer anytime we entered someone's house, and once they found out that we, too, were believers, they insisted that we pray as many times as possible. Also, everywhere we went, we were greeted by people with a polite-style of handshake where the right hand is extended while the left hand holds onto the right forearm. Because of this display of courtesy it sometimes took us more than thirty minutes to walk across this village the size of half a football field. At every house we entered, an enormous amount of food was placed before us. There were walnuts, various stir fried dishes, the thick doughy rice cakes, hard-boiled eggs, peanuts, sunflower seeds, sugar cane, pumpkin, and an untold number of bananas. So, at our first house we

126

made the mistake of eating our fill in order to show our appreciation. However, little did we know that we were to visit nearly every house in the village and that the same things would be set before us each time! Needless to say, we were quite lethargic during most of our stay. (Next time we'll know to eat just a little at each place.)

Eventually, they decided that we should stay at the church elder's house, and we fell into hard sleep around 9 p.m.

**Christmas Day, Dec. 25—third day out**

Since it is Christmas Day, and they believe that Jesus was born in the early morning, we arose at about 4:30 a.m. to go to a church service. Afterwards, we were encouraged to go back to sleep, which, of course, we did.

Later, that morning, we played some basketball (every village seems to have a dirt court and a couple broken-down goals), and went about with the same routine of going from house to house, eating, and asking as many questions as we thought would be polite.

Later that afternoon, I felt the Father saying that we should meet together privately as a team to see how everyone felt, considering the last couple days' events. So we asked permission to leave for a little while, and headed down the trail a ways to pray and share our thoughts about possible options for the next few days. I believe most of us were wanting to head out as soon as possible to the next place, but I knew that God was telling me that we should stay at least one more night.

What I really felt was that He wanted to teach us about patience in this area, and He soon confirmed that this was the right decision. Within the next couple of hours, we found ourselves once again in a small bamboo hut at the other end of the village. As we were sitting there, we heard some people up the hill singing to the tune "Blessed Assurance." We sang it again in English. Then, as L. translated, J. told a moving story about a pastor in Romania who had sung that song while being beaten in prison, and then, many years later, learned that people had heard him singing and had become believers as a result. The four or five people in the hut all sighed with astonishment after the story was finished. Then they began to ask more questions:

"Did Jesus ever go to America?"

"What country was He from?"

"Was He as noble and righteous as Mao Ze Dong?"

Most of the people in the room were of either the younger and middle-aged generation.

It soon became clear that hardly any of them had read any part of the Bible and none had ever been discipled. We happened to have two video CDs of the *JESUS Film* in the most commonly spoken indigenous language, and we asked if they wanted to see it. Of course, they said "Yes!" When we started this video, we found out that they could understand every word of it. Within a matter of minutes, we left the hut because it was filled with about thirty or forty people crowded around the little five inch screen of our portable player. We had to change the batteries out about half-way through, and it wouldn't play the very end of the film, but I know that their curiosity was piqued. Both of us will be more prepared next time we come to this village. This storying format is definitely the way to go in discipling the believers of this area. That night, we went to sleep to the sound of a group of carolers going from house to house.

## Dec. 26—fourth day out

The next morning was spent doing the same

things, and by afternoon they finally allowed us to go up to the next village. They insisted on sending us with an escort to introduce us to the next village elder. It took about one hour to reach the village, and it's the largest village in this area with more than three hundred families.

Once again, nearly 80 percent of the people claim to be followers of Jesus, and you can imagine how long it took simply to walk down the street of such a place! We once again engaged in the polite tradition of going from house to house, but, thankfully, this time it only included the village leaders and elders, as it would have been impossible to make the rounds to everyone's house. We once again showed a large portion of the *JESUS Film*, and they were once again overjoyed to hear something in their own heart language. They had a large dance that night that imitated many of their agricultural motions. Afterwards, we slept in the village elder's house.

## Dec. 27—fifth day out

We spent the morning going from house to house, and in the early afternoon J. and I became the star attraction during the basketball games. It seems that during this time all the surrounding villagers from neighboring villages come here to engage in games. Afterward, a policeman from a nearby post came to check our ID's. Before leaving he thanked us, and assured everyone that he'd done this for our own "safety." He also told L. how the religious situation of this area is "complicated." That's a big "Hmm...."

Later that evening the elders had a special program put together for us. We watched, along with the rest of the village, as men and women of all ages performed in the village square. Many wore traditional dress and danced traditional dances, as the musicians beat the drums and played the flute. It turned out that we also were a part of the program. A guitar appeared, and we sang a couple praise songs. As L. translated, we found out that many of the dances had a Christian meaning. There was even one song about Christmas that was said to last for three days! We only got the fifteen minute version. We slept hard that night.

### Dec 28—sixth day out

Of course, they insisted that we stay one more day, but we didn't want to impose on them any longer.

So, we began to pack up our stuff as breakfast was being prepared.

It was during this time that several men came in from a village about sixty to seventy kilometers away. They claimed to be believers and to want any material that we had to offer. They especially wanted the *JESUS Film* that was in their indigenous language, "to take to other villages so they can believe in Jesus also!" We were all floored by this statement. We were ecstatic, but we had already given our only two local-language films to the village leaders at each place we had stayed. They gave us their names and showed us on the map where they lived. We promised to revisit them with their desired material. Our Father had truly answered far and above more than we had

135

ever asked for on this trip, and my faith in timing is increased all the more!

After breakfast, we happened to catch a truck leaving from the village to the nearest market town. We jumped in the back and spent much of the way down the mountain singing common praise songs with other local passengers from the village. In about two hours we were in a decent hotel with hot showers, spending the rest of the day in rest and thanksgiving to our Father.

## CHAPTER SIX

# HEARING AND OBEYING GOD'S VOICE

In e-mails to supporters back in the States, I am always expressing how thankful I am for their prayers. I can't talk about that enough. Prayer is so important to me, because it is so much more than supplication to a powerful Being, asking for protection from harm. To me, it is conversation. It is part of the relationship between the Creator and the created. God is a communicator God. All throughout the Bible, He is talking to his people.

I was taught from a young age to talk to God. I

can't remember ever questioning His presence or His ability to answer my prayers. I know the thinking and teaching that we've all heard about prayer, and how God answers: "Sometimes it is wait, sometimes it is no, and sometimes He answers immediately."

Honestly, I have had so many experiences where God answered me quickly. I like that, especially since there are many times I am in tense situations that require immediate and sound judgments. Having conversations with God continually puts that into practice – you learn to hear the voice of the Savior.

I try to maintain an attitude of prayer all throughout my day. I talk to God quietly when in the presence of other people and aloud when I'm by myself. Many times I ask, "What do I do now?" or, "What is your will in this matter?" Many times while out on the trail, I'll just talk aloud to God by reading His Word back to him or just chat. We have a common everyday conversation. It's a great way to pass the time on a long hike. I've had WA ask me if I talk to God and if He talks back to me. I say, "yes" to both questions. They will often ask what His voice sounds like. They will ask, "Is it the voice of an animal or man?" I know it sounds simple, but communication with the Lord doesn't have to be in King James English or in perfect English or Chinese grammar. Some of the most meaningful moments I've had in prayer were during simple times of confession, when I say, "God, I'm sorry for my sin. Please forgive me and give me strength never to do that again." I'm so glad I can bring my needs before Him. He never tires of my petitioning him for answers. Often I talk to him on behalf of my family and friends. I have discovered that even when I'm angry, I can tell Him how I feel and He ministers to me.

He often reminds me that some of His choicest servants struggled with sin and disobedience. The difference was their willingness to repent and move forward.

I'm so glad our God isn't like the gods created by man. He is a God who knows me and knows me thoroughly through and through. Prayer has helped me to see my need for Him and to discover my dependence upon Him. On one particular trip, I learned a valuable lesson about being obedient to what God is telling me to do. It changed my entire outlook on how I do my ministry and how I need to be more sensitive to God's Spirit when He tells me to do something.

Medical volunteer trips have served as an awesome inroad to our people group. The WA are impoverished and lack even the basic medical services. Every time we make return trips to Kawa villages, we hear of children who have died from malnutrition and illnesses that could have been so easily combated. Dental services are also a hot draw in most of the villages. Many adults have those sets of teeth that would serve perfectly on a poster that parents could use for their kids – "You want to know why you have to brush? Take a look at this...." The doctors who have come through with us – and even the volunteers who are medical novices – all participate in dental clinics. These clinics consist mostly of yanking out rotten teeth. I've had to jump in there, as well, and help out with this. They see us come into their village, and they know we're there to help them. In one village we trekked to, an old woman came up to me, and, without a word, sat down, leaned her head back and opened her mouth. She had black, spoiled teeth. The pain must have been killing her. I yanked her teeth out, and she went away smiling. It didn't matter a bit to her that I had no medical experience. That's not something I shared with her, either.

Neli was just a young man in his early twenties who lived in a remote village in the mountains.

Some time before, one of our medical volunteer groups had hiked through his village. Neli's health had become a serious consideration to some of our team – he had been diagnosed with tuberculosis. All he needed was some simple medication that by Western standards was cheap. Since his family had no money to make the purchase, our team bought the medicine for him and started him on the six-month regimen. The team shared the Gospel with Neli and even presented him with his own Bible. He could read and showed great interest as his health also began to improve as the medicine began to work. We prayed for Neli daily and asked the Lord to heal him. Our team made several trips through Neli's village prior to the medical team's visit. On the day our medical team arrived, Neli helped us so much and served as a great person of peace. His influence with his village was incredible. Everyone liked Neli, and the villagers liked our team because of the medicine we had provided and the kindness we had showed to one of their own.

People in the village were open to the Gospel, and we had good reputation. But this is where our team really missed it. Even though Neli showed interest in following Jesus, no one ever asked, "Neli, today would you like to pray and receive Christ into your heart?" There seems to be a thought that there is plenty of time for people to come to Christ. Or, that they will come when they are ready. This idea of "our timing" is so wrong. It is the Holy Spirit who draws and convicts. The Bibles states,

"Today is the day of salvation…" Hebrews 3:7

As the Holy Spirit says, "If you hear God speak today, don't be stubborn. Today is the day of salvation!"

That night as our medical team bedded down in the village, Neli was near me helping spread out sleeping mats and working on the fire. I felt the Lord urging me to ask him some questions about his understanding of what it means to follow Christ. I asked if he understood the Gospel. "Yes," he said. I asked him if he was willing to repent of his sins and ask God to come into his life and save him. To this, he said that he wasn't sure. At that moment, the man who was designated as the leader of our group said he felt that I was too aggressive and should back off pressing for a deci-

145

sion from Neli. As we talked about it, my friend felt concerned that if Neli came to Christ first in the village, he would experience a lot of pressure from the rest of the villagers because of how friendly we were with him —as if he were making a commitment to just stay in our favor. I was reluctant to back off, but did anyway.

That was a restless night for me. I just never could rest. I went to sleep that night wondering what had happened. Didn't I hear the voice of the Holy Spirit, urging me to speak the truth to Neli? In my heart, I knew I had caved in and should have pressed a little bit further in spite of my team leader asking me to stop.

The next morning we packed up and moved on to

our next location. It was some weeks later we learned what had happened after we left Neli's village. Within a few hours of our team's departure, Neli started to cough severely. His coughing was so violent that a blood vessel in his neck burst. He dropped dead in front of his house where we had held our clinic just twelve hours earlier.

Our young friend was dead, and he slipped into eternity without Christ. That young man is in hell at this moment because of my lack of sensitivity to his spiritual need. When our team sat down and discussed this situation, we came to the understanding and awareness that Neli's blood was on our hands.

"So when you stretch out your hands {in prayer},
I will turn my eyes away from you. Even though

you offer many prayers,

I will not listen because your hands are covered

with blood." Isaiah 1:15

We would give an account of our failure some day. It was a difficult lesson to learn, and Neli is paying for it for all of eternity.

I look back on that event and conclude there were several things I could have done, should have done differently. The first is that I should have been obedient to what God was leading me to do. I should have continued to talk to Neli into the wee hours of the morning if necessary just to answer his questions about coming to faith in Christ. I could have given a public invitation earlier in the day when we were providing medical care for the entire village. Maybe Neli would have responded to the Gospel in a group setting if he saw others stepping out as well. Other things come to my mind, but the fact is – Neli is dead and our team didn't do all that was humanly possible to win him to Christ. It is important for me to point out here that since that time, we have been faithful to give public invitations for people to put their faith in Christ. My team member who spoke to me that night and asked me to back off talking to Neli stands right beside me. He has learned the local dialect, and we will preach in two different languages. And people will respond. Some valuable lessons can be painful. I am so thankful we serve such a gracious God who doesn't strike us down for our foolishness.

# CHAPTER SEVEN

# BEING A STRATEGIC KINGDOM PLAYER

# HOW DO WE DO IT?

I am a Strategy Coordinator for an unreached people group. A lot of people don't understand this task. I'm not sure I did either when I first accepted the job assignment. In some of my first training meetings (Yuck! What a dirty word!), there were these "10 Principles" that I was given to review. They really helped me understand some of what I was to do in approaching my mission task in the right frame of mind. These principles ring true for anyone who is sold out to the Lordship of Christ and who is committed to answering that call that resonates deep in their soul. These stand true regardless of age, gender, or place in this world.

Work among unreached peoples supersedes any organization. It is a way of life for people who have committed their heart and soul to a passion and a vision of reaching a lost and dying world with the saving message of Jesus Christ. Our vision is illustrated by the scriptural imagery of all peoples gathered together, bowing in worship before Christ's throne. We exist solely to bring the light of Christ to the lost: to the least evangelized, to the disenfranchised, and to those living in corners of the globe utterly void of any gospel witness. God's Word guarantees the ultimate victory.

Chew on these thoughts. I don't intend for anything to sound canned or preachy, but if you're determined to grab that heavenly blueprint and start asking God to help you formulate an action plan, these are some good points to keep in mind.

## Destination is the point, and you are the key!

An indigenous church planting movement among every people must be the point of all we do. Plans, programs and technology are not our foremost consideration, but only a means to the end. You as a worker among unreached peoples and your competency and character are the key in reaching the destination. Therefore, we must do all we can to provide adequate support, training, and guidance. God calls many laborers to work in His vineyard. Many hear the call, but few respond. Taking this a step further, entrance into service isn't enough either. It is obedience and performance that counts. The destination for me is seeing a movement of God among the WA people group. By accepting God's calling, I become a key part in their coming to know Christ.

## We must continually change

The unreached world is an ever-changing world of governments and forces that are violently resisting Gospel witness. Our willingness to challenge and to change the way we do things has been one of our chief strengths. Unwillingness to challenge what has become status quo or conventional wisdom will mean stagnation. Thus, we must continually check our course, making minor adjustments and even major changes. The way we did things fifty years ago – wow! even fifteen years ago – is vastly different from how things work today. Things evolve as new challenges are discovered, much like peeling back layers of an onion. Men and methods often change, but the message never does. If I'm not growing, I'm dying.

## Organizational conformity for the sake of conformity is death

Our Lord has created something unique and distinctive in each of us for the sake of the nations. To sacrifice the nations on the altar of organizational convenience or uniformity is wrong. We are part of a larger family, but we do not have to look or act exactly like our brothers and sisters. Our motivation must not be conformity to organizational standards, procedures and policies. Rather, our motives must be driven by what it will take to reach the nations, not by what it will take to strengthen the name of our organization.

Don't strive to be like anything or anyone, except for being conformed to the likeness of Jesus. We are all unique. God's creativity is wonderful. If I conform to some person or shape my strategy for winning the WA to Christ on the basis of someone else's plan, I may miss what God wants for me.

**The way forward for World "A" Workers must be through humility and service**

The vision and passion which we share for the nations and which we believe to be the very heart of our God will not be grasped by others through our arrogance or power of persuasion, but only

155

through our humility and service to the rest of the Christian community. Since the politics of power and turf wars are not the way of our Lord, they should not be our way, either. We must continually remember that we participate in taking The Edge only at our Lord's gracious invitation. Several years ago while standing on a mountain in China looking at all the villages dotting the landscape, God told me, "The edge is where I take you! For some missionaries the edge is an unreached city, for me, it is an unreached people group. Something else about the edge that has stayed with me is that no matter where I put my head for the night, the next morning I realize God moved the edge. Today the edge is here! Tomorrow the edge is somewhere else. Putting it plainly, our lives should reflect the words of Jesus, when he said,

"The Son of Man came not to be served, but to serve." If I begin conversations with local WA believers, local unbelieving villagers or even other missionaries with the phrase, "What can I do for you?" it makes a lot of difference.

## We all live under authority and are accountable

We live together under the covenant to bless the nations. In this relationship we mentor, correct, teach and support each other. Thus, all of us are accountable to someone in a linear, corporate-like structure in which individuals under authority are empowered for appropriate decision-making and leadership. We don't take votes, and we don't establish committees. The context in which we work and the stewardship of resources demand that we operate in the most efficient, effective manner possible.

## The greater our diversity, the greater our strength

A leveling of everyone to the lowest common denominator is not our aim. Everyone must not look and act the same. Equity is not our way of operating. Everyone will be treated differently. Our aim must be to maximize everyone's unique gifts and personality so that the destination is reached.

## Communication must be wide and secure

We must redouble our efforts and use the latest means in order to communicate effectively and securely with each other and our constituency. This may not mean a great deal to you now, but consider this. If you're planning on going to a remote part of the world where the people have never had the opportunity to hear the Gospel, why do you think they are in that condition? More often than not, it's because of a severe isolation. Many times it's because of political forces resistant to outside influence. If you're going to dive in and work among these people, you had better have a system in place that will allow you to communicate with "your" world without compromising what you're doing.

## The Edge is where we belong

As individuals and as a group, we dare not draw back from the edge of the unreached. We are people who are gifted for and called to the edge; thus, we must continue to enter new people groups and cities rather than seeking only to consolidate the gains we've made. We are about pioneering. Going after the lost. Pushing forward into spiritual darkness. Years ago as I was thinking about the "edge," it came into my mind that some people live and work in the cities while others work in the rural areas. In every case where God's people are obeying Him, they are in His will. So, "the edge" is where God takes me.

**We will do whatever it takes to get to the destination**

This does not mean that the end justifies every means. Rather, it means that we do what our Lord has asked of us, believing that He intends for His church to exist among all peoples before He returns. To get to this destination, we must move beyond restrictive thinking, work with Christian brothers and sisters around the world, and believe He is working in every situation. We are seeing this today with the loss of life among missionaries who are being murdered for no reason other than their faith in the Lord Jesus and their desire to bind up wounds and minister to the brokenhearted. Members of my short-term extreme teams have always said, "Dude, whatever it takes" when I outline some of the dangers they could encounter on the hostile trail. I believe they mean it. Many of them have returned to the States now and are finishing seminary or other training in preparation to return to the field.

## The organization is not your God (or your mother)

Your call is from the One who called Abraham to

161

be a blessing to the nations. Your dependency must rest in Him alone. Your power does not lie in the organization's resources or name, but in the One who created all things. If our worship and allegiance is not focused singularly on the One who made all peoples and on His Son, then we disqualify ourselves from this race. God and God alone is God. The mission organization I am a part of is perhaps the best mission organization in the world, but they are not God. If I look only to the organization to meet my needs and shift my focus off the Lord, my faith is warped. God uses the organization to meet the needs of my family, but the company isn't my mother or God. As much as I love what we stand for and what we do as a body of missionaries, my first love and allegiance is to the Savior.

***Complete the Task*** – Nothing else! The command of Christ compels us to go to the lost of this world. The task of evangelization rests in our obedience to this command.

Old WA man telling the story of taking a head

# APPENDIX A

# WHAT OTHERS ARE SAYING

"People will say: 'Oh, it's too hard. You shouldn't go on that kind of trip. You should just send your money.' I have had people say that to me before I left," said **Tucker**, a caretaker at a Christian youth camp. "It's easy to say that in the safety of your own bubble. But now that I'm here, standing on this mountain, I realize that there is no way that Guy could have done this all by himself. He needed this team to help him. It's such a difficult concept to grasp, coming from the American perspective of a church on every corner," Tucker adds. "You read about places like this. It's almost overwhelming to be here in a place completely de-void of the Gospel."

**John** said he came to the mountains of East Asia out of obedience and a desire to see God at work. Despite his inexperience in hiking, the forty-seven year-old maintenance engineer said, "God took care of everything, and it was all worthwhile to see that man sitting in the dirt [watching the Gospel being presented]. I've never seen a more literal, down-to-earth example of Jesus' teaching in my life."

Dr. **Charles**, a team physician on one trip, began casting down the stones of the sacrificial altars he would see on the trail. "This is my second time to be here, and I will cast down a stone every time I visit this place," he said. Charles, at sixty-five years of age, is a great man of God.

"This was a very difficult trip," **Alan** admitted. "But God provided for our every need. When we were out of water and struggling to make it up a hill – not knowing if there was a stream on the other side – God sustained us. If we don't go, who will? Of course it's hard – but so was walking up Golgotha. These people need to hear the Gospel. More memorable than all the scenery and sweat", Alan said, "is the fact that someone will be impacted for eternity because we came. God gave us His example, and we followed. It's as simple as that."

Alan also said, "It doesn't take a theological degree, and it's not about being a super Christian. It's about being obedient to the command Christ gave His church. If you believe the Word of God – to love your neighbor as yourself – how can you not do something about it? The gospel that we've been given is not a complex thing. You can take a stick and scratch in the dirt and make men who have never heard understand that they need God [in order] to be blessed in their lives. You don't have to be a biblical scholar to do that. We've learned that this week."

"Seeing how these people live, it makes me feel so wasteful", said **Josh**, a twenty year-old student who works in an outfitter store. "I live in a nice house and drive a good car; I live the good life. They live in huts and work to the bone just to get through the day. I don't know why God has given me what He has. I'll never be the same after this trip. This experience impacts for a lifetime. Somehow, I wish people could feel in their hearts what I do. We're here to worship God – that is what missions is to me. That is what I want to do with my life."

"After hiking up and down the mountainous terrain for hours, dabbing the sweat away from his forehead with a bandanna, S.O. Guy turned to our team and jokingly said, 'I'm too old for this'," **Lin** recalled. The saying was hilarious. The surroundings were breathtakingly beautiful. What made the saying so hilarious was that the whole team was most likely suffering from excessive sweating and muscle aches the same way S.O. Guy was. Yet with the sweating, muscle aches, and hours of trek-king, the target village was still peeking through the bamboo on the other mountain. We had been in similar situations many times before as a team. Humor helps greatly with tough hikes to reach the villages of the WA people. Something else S.O. Guy said that really made a deep impression on me was mentioned as we were talking about how long it would take to reach a particular isolated village on the top of a steep mountain. "That's why they are an unreached people group." The short saying so aptly describes a main reason behind the lost-ness of the people and at the same time sums up the challenges the field workers face.

# APPENDIX B

# TIPS FOR THE EDGERS

Think you want to join us on the edge? Dive in! There's no better time than now to join in the harvest. For those who are interested in going to the edge in ways you've read about in this book, don't be discouraged if you can't find the assignment that strikes a chord in your heart. Keep digging! They're out there! There are hundreds of remote people groups that have never been touched with the Gospel – go find them! You are hearing from a missionary's heart. I am passionate for what I am able to do for the Kingdom of God. As fired up as you may interpret me to be, always remember how the heart of God is even more focused on the world and turned toward the heart of the repentant.

As you search for the trailhead to jump off on, here are some things to consider as you're getting ready:

# 1

Don't be afraid to train hard, and don't just get physically fit for the trail:

Prepare your heart,

Prepare your body,

Prepare your spirit.

# 2

Don't be made afraid by what you see on the news or in the newspapers. *Veggie-Tales* had it right when they sang "God is bigger than the boogie-man! He's bigger than Godzilla or the monsters on TV! Oh, God is bigger than the boogie-man, and He's watching out for you and me!" The news will report on chaos and turmoil all over the world. You need to be concerned about where God wants you. Obedience.

# 3

Make sure you have the proper nutrition, such as a

high-carbohydrate diet. Eat well and take good vitamins.

# 4

Once on the trail, look ahead and keep your eyes focused.

Be alert to physical dangers.

Be sensitive to spiritual encounters.

# 5

Be prepared for all conditions.

Bring the proper clothing and food.

Bring spiritually enriching music and your pocket Bible.

# 6

Make sure you drink plenty of fluids. The trail can be hot and long.

Water for your body satisfies your thirst, but always remember John 4: 10-14: Jesus answered her, "If you knew the gift of God and who it is that asks you for a drink, you would have asked him and he would have given you living water." "Sir," the woman said, "you have nothing to draw with and the well is deep. Where can you get this living water? Are you greater than our father Jacob, who gave us the well and drank from it himself, as did also his sons and his flocks and herds?" Jesus answered, "Everyone who drinks this water will be thirsty again, but whoever drinks the water I give him will never thirst. Indeed, the water I give him will become in him a spring of water welling up to eternal life."

Jesus satisfies the soul, and this is a truth you will need to communicate to those you meet, but it also applies very much to us.

# 7

Have your equipment in good mechanical order. Repair damage prior to arrival. This goes for your mind and body, as well.

Mental and emotional problems are not going to get better on the mission field.

We train ourselves so well to pay attention to tangible things – when our boots are getting worn, when a rope gets frayed – let's pay attention to the spiritual, as well.

# 8

Get advice from others who have done what you are about to do and from those who have been where you are about to go.

A testimony is good for the heart and soul.

# 9

Join a prayer group.

Meet with others who are like-minded regularly for fellowship and encouragement.

# 10

Have fun.

It's important not to take yourself too seriously.

Be intense without going overboard.

Go as hard as you can without stressing yourself and those who also serve on the same team.

Explaining the Gospel

The author sharing with a volunteer
team before their exit from China

# ABOUT THE AUTHOR

C. Brandt Smith, Jr.
1910 Scenic Road
JONESBORO, ARKANSAS 72401

C. Brandt Smith, Jr. is widely known and used across America. He is in constant demand as a public speaker. He has a unique ability to use his ready wit not only to entertain but also to drive home truths from the Bible. His experiences while traveling and living in numerous cultures other than his own beloved United States of America have helped shape his personality and worldview.

He and wife Gailia have been married twenty-four years and have four children. Their two sons and two daughters are not too mixed up from having lived abroad most of their lives.

Brandt and Gailia served as missionaries for more than twelve years. The Mandarin Chinese language is their second language and has been a major part of their ability to connect with nationals while living in China, Taiwan and Thailand. Their work has taken them to nearly every country in East and Southeast Asia.

He has been very active in producing the Following Jesus Mandarin version of the Chronological Oral Bible. Readers are encouraged to investigate this project at www.fjseries.org for more information.

He has served as pastor of three Southern Baptist churches and as visiting adjunct professor of missions at the Mid-America Baptist Theological Seminary in Germantown, Tennessee.

Currently, he is completing his Ph.D. in Leadership and serving the congregation of Walnut Street Baptist Church in Jonesboro, Arkansas as associate pastor.

# LOOK OUT FOR THE HEADHUNTERS

C. BRANDT SMITH, JR.